ADAM's CALENDA

Discovering the Oldest Man-made Structure on Earth.

75,000 years ago…
early humans built a stone calendar that predates all other stone structures found to date. Who were they? Why did they need a calendar?

By Johan Heine & Michael Tellinger

Adam's Calendar

A book by Michael Tellinger

Inspired by Johan Heine in 2007.
This is Edition 2021

Published by Zulu Planet Publishers
PO Box 204, Waterval Boven, 1195
South Africa

Copyright © Michael Tellinger

Contact:
publisher@zuluplanet.com
Website: www.michaeltellinger.com

Layout and Cover: Deep Fried Design
peter@deepfried.co.za

Photographs by Johan Heine and Michael Tellinger
Images of the crash and rescue mission were provided by Mimi Brodie. This includes the first photo ever taken of the calendar site after its rediscovery by Johan Heine.

All rights reserved.
No part of this book may be copied, reproduced, recorded, broadcast, transmitted or stored in any way or manner, by any means or by any technology, in existence now or in the future, without prior written permission from the publisher.

Books by Michael Tellinger:
Slave Species of god
Slave Species of the Gods
Adam's Calendar
Temples of the African Gods
African Temples of the Anunnaki
UBUNTU Contributionism

GEOLOGICAL REPORT

The site occurs in an area where dolerite is abundant. This means that the rocks have not been imported from far, but most likely manipulated into various orientations, and possibly worked and chipped for the correct effect. The cliffs in the vicinity are predominantly sandstone from the Transvaal Supergoup and protected by the more resistant and extremely hard dolerite sill, on which the site occurs. The orientation and appearance of the monoliths at the site are distinctly different from the other occurrences of the dolerite both north and south of the site. Certain parts of the monoliths appear to have been shaped or worked to get a desired effect such as that seen on the "stone man". Determining an age from the weathering of the surface of these rock is very difficult as past climates would have played a significant role in the rate of weathering. It is however clear that they have been exposed to the elements for thousands of years based on the extensive erosion patterns on some of the rocks.

Dr Dion Brandt
Consulting geologist, Barberton, South Africa.

The Authors

Johan Heine and Michael Tellinger after the first weekend of exploring the calendar site and planning their new book.

The Founder

Johan Heine is a pilot and explorer by heart. As the head of the fire fighting unit in the forests of Mpumalanga, South Africa, he has been flying over this beautiful mountainous part of the world and exploring it for 20 years. It would be accurate to say that he knows it like the back of his hand. But it was only when he was called out to assist in the search for a colleague who had crashed in the mountains, that he made a discovery that will change how we view our human history. At the edge of a mountain top, he spotted a strange arrangement of giant rocks. Upon his

ACKNOWLEDGMENTS

Numerous colleagues and friends have contributed directly and indirectly in achieving the objective of bringing the secrets of the Mpumalanga ruins to the attention of the world. I would like to extend special thanks to the following researchers and open minded people who have assisted and supported me in living out my dream of discovering the truths of life, ancient history and the ruins. Cyril Hromnik, Willemien Hodgekinson, Michael Tellinger, Jim Murray, Richard Wade, Willem Olivier, Nico Heyns, Isak Barnard, Paul van Niekerk, Chris Austin, Louis Venter, David van Wyk, At Oosthuizen, Johan Zietsman, Anthony Stevens and Peter Delius. And, especially, my wife Lizette and our two daughters, Lizane and Ruzane, who poured coffee from the flask, took photographs, held up sheets of paper and got up very early to support my dream.

Johan Heine

return and closer inspection, this stone calendar site has turned out to be the oldest known man-made site on Earth.

For 4 years Johan had been pondering, plotting and photographing his historic discovery. After many attempts to attract the interest of historians and archaeologists had failed, he never gave up his quest to measure the site and establish the ancient and original geographical alignments. His persistence has resulted in discovering the oldest man-made structure on Earth and bringing real significance to the earliest humans that emerged in southern Africa.

Introduction

The *Johan Heine Stone Calendar* (affectionately called Adam's Calendar) has been dated by astronomer Bill Hollenbach to be between 25,000 and 150,000 years old. We would place the actual date closer to around 75,000 years, based on the movement of the peoples in southern Africa and the emergence of rock art during that period. But it could in fact be even older – dating back to the dawn of Homo sapiens some 250,000 years ago.

A close-up view of Adam's Calendar on a summer's day 2007. Notice the top of the rock on the left that broke off at some distant time – lying in the foreground next to its parent rock.

The moon rises as the sun sets over the calendar. Could the ancient people and architects of the site have used the movement of the moon as well as the sun to measure time and other events? The site seems to hold many more secrets that will be examined and hopefully answered in years to come.

Afternoon shadows from other strategically placed rocks fall on the monoliths. Notice how the rocks lean over towards the cliff edge, as a result of the top layer of soil slowly sliding towards the cliff edge over many millennia.

The sun setting between the 2 main monolith rocks. Just one of many magical moments for any visitor to behold. The notion that humans were observing the movement of the sun in this spot for over 75,000 years leaves one somewhat dumbfounded. Who were these people and where did they suddenly get the knowledge to build stone calendar structures such as this? But more importantly, why did these early humans suddenly have the need to build a calendar?

AFRICAN MYTHS AND LEGENDS

There is an overwhelming consensus by scholars, academics and even mystics that southern Africa is the cradle of humankind and that this is where the first humans walked the Earth before migrating to the distant corners of our planet.

Through the study of mitochondrial DNA in females, geneticist Wesley Brown of the Howard Goodman Laboratory found a staggering bit of evidence that points to a time when the first humans suddenly appeared on Earth, reigniting the ongoing debate about the 'missing link'.

His calculation shows that the common ancestor to all humans appeared somewhere between 180,000 and 360,000 years ago. She was affectionately called Mitochondrial Eve. The amazing coincidence is that genetic studies on the Y-chromosome in males have shown very similar results.

This had a twofold effect. Those anthropologists that support evolution now had a real challenge to find the so-called missing link, while others who support the concept of creation had a strong argument that there was an actual point in time when mankind was first created. Needless to say, the argument still continues today.

While new discoveries are being made by scientists to support the scale of evolution, religious philosophers are decoding some of the mysterious stories from the many religions on Earth.

The fact remains, that southern Africa holds some of the deepest mysteries in all of human history.

Because, while much has been written about the first humans who appeared in this part of the world, we have found very little evidence of their activity or what they did and what kind of lives they led.

**Who were these first humans?
What did they do?
How did they live?
Where did they disappear to?**

The first signs of human intelligence and consciousness only appeared around 75 000 years ago, when the Khoisan people of southern Africa, sometimes also referred to as Bushmen, started leaving behind an array of spectacular cave paintings all over this part of the continent. Finely crafted beads and bracelet fragments found in a cave at Blombos in the Western Cape, South Africa, show that these early humans had already developed a feel for the arts and crafts.

Adam's Calendar | 11

Deep grooves carved by early humans into dolerite monoliths. These are some of the hardest rocks on earth. The strategically placed monoliths lie scattered along the entire mountain ridge like a stone graveyard trapped in time. Hiding many ancient secrets from the most distant times in human history.

A gold prospector's claim from sometime in the 19th century. Indicating that this region is just one of many hundreds that has had gold mining activity dating back from a hundred years ago to many thousands of years in the past. Many ancient gold mines lie hidden in the surrounding mountains.

The legends become even more vivid when we learn about the great empire of Monomotapa whose kings were powerful and wealthy in gold. When we move to around 1000 BC we encounter the mysterious Queen Sheba who ruled a kingdom in the lost land of Ophir, teeming with endless supplies of gold; and the wise and wealthy king Solomon who seduced Queen Sheba and obtained all his gold from her.

Adventurers and historians have been searching for evidence of these lost lands and civilisations for centuries in the hope of discovering some of these riches themselves, with no luck. While these characters and stories are mostly biblical, we need to examine their historical relevance.

**Is it possible that there really was such a place?
Was it really filled with limitless wealth in gold?
Was it here where the wealthiest kings on Earth got their gold?**

Rock samples containing a range of minerals that inspired the prospector to stake his claim.

Small rocks trapped in protruding invasive lava rock formation.

An ancient mine with a possible grave in the foreground. There are a few more graves further up the side of the mine. Based on the burial method this is a more recent mine probably only several hundred years old.

The mountainsides are filled with hundreds of excavated depressions such as these, now filled with soil forming a fertile place for trees to grow. In ancient times, this was most probably the preferred technique to get to the golden ore contained in the mountain bedrock. Is it a coincidence that Sheba Gold Mine is located a short distance from here? Still one of the richest gold mines in the world after 150 years of mining!

Many speculations have been thrown about by all and sundry about the land of Ophir, its location and the whereabouts of Queen Sheba. Most of these speculations tend to point to southern Africa as its most likely location. And why not?

This is after all the place where most of the gold in the world has been mined in modern history, and it was no different in ancient times. Is it a coincidence that the richest gold mine in the world today, Sheba Gold Mine, is located right here in Mpumalanga, South Africa?

If this was indeed the land of Ophir from where King Solomon got all his gold, it stands to reason that there must have been a high level of gold mining going on for quite some time before Solomon tapped into it. And this is only the beginning of what seems to be a long history of mining and slavery that spanned for many thousands of years.

Who were those people that knew how to extract gold from ore?
Where did they get their knowledge and skills from? What happened to them?

A RICH AND DIVERSE HISTORY

In the heart of southern Africa lies the scattered evidence of a lost civilisation whose people built some 20,000 stone structures. These breathtaking ruins constitute the largest continuous stone settlement ever built on Earth as it stretches over thousands of kilometres from South Africa all the way to Kenya and beyond. These mysterious ancient ruins consist of dwellings, forts, temples, roads, irrigation systems and agricultural terraces that cover thousands of square kilometres. It is our estimate that more stone went into building these features than went into building all of the Egyptian pyramids. It is an archaeologist's dream that will unveil even greater and more mysterious secrets in years to come.

Historian explorer Dr Cyril Hromnik (right) describing the significance of this ancient Hindu altar from the Dravidian period in Indian history, to Jim Murray. Mpumalanga contains many such altars of various sizes. This is one of the best preserved examples discovered to date, indicating a wide presence of Indian gold miners in southern Africa dating back to the birth of Christ or even further back in time.

Another example of an Indian altar situated inside a stone structure with astronomical alignments. This altar is clearly positioned to face west, indicated by the large marker stone in the distance.

Side view of the intricate and meticulously constructed dwellings in close proximity to the gold mines and other stone structures that seem to have more spiritual and astronomic observational purpose.

This stone dwelling seems to have a grave in the centre from more recent times.

Example of mine workers' stone dwellings near a gold mine hidden in the distance.

Whoever built these dwellings had a good understanding of insulation. This was no quick-fix solution to erect a home and it is clear that the builders were here to stay for a long time. The walls are on average over 60 cm wide, consisting of large rocks forming the outer layers, with smaller stones filling the cavity between them. The roof or 'superstructure' has long disappeared but evidence of it may lie beneath the soil.

The remaining walls of some ruins are still over 2,5 metres tall, indicating its original height.

When historians first researched these structures they simply assumed that they were cattle kraals left behind by the Bantu people as they moved south and settled the land from around the 13th century. But research work done by people like Cyril Hromnik, Richard Wade, Johan Heine and a handful of others over the past twenty years, into ancient southern African history, has revealed that these stone structures are in fact the remains of ancient temples and astronomical observatories of many lost ancient civilisations that stretch back for many thousands of years.

Just a few examples of the many thousands of circular stone structures that make up the largest concentration of stone structures on Earth. An estimated 20,000 of these ancient structures are spread over 4000 kilometres from South Africa to Kenya and beyond. Many of these show an intricate understanding of geographic positioning and astronomical alignment. Some have intricate geometric formulas and calculations worked into their shapes.

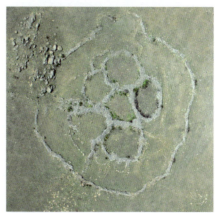

Intricate Reiki symbols and Phi ratios (Golden ratio) make up the structure of some ruins.

Adam's Calendar | 21

A view from the north marker towards the south marker dissecting the two main monoliths.

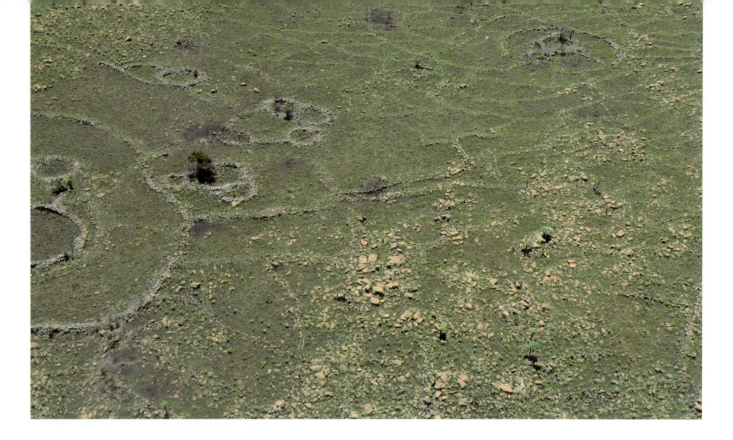

THE FIRST CITY ON EARTH

Despite the erosion, aerial images display the evidence of sprawling extended settlements, structures and terraces that join up over vast distances.

This ruin displays a well know Hindu symbol of fertility.

One of the world's finest archaeologists and broad thinkers, Richard Wade, has linked these circular ruins of southern Africa to what would today be called Arabic and Chinese traders from thousands of years ago. But Wade goes even further than Hromnik, by suggesting that the presence of Indian gold miners in this part of the world can be linked to the early Harappan civilisation of the Indus Valley some 2500 BC. This clearly supports the finds of Cyril Hromnik who has in many ways been ridiculed for his findings by the establishments of South African academia.

It is curious to find that many of these ruins are designed with ancient Hindu symbolism and some even have Arabic wording carefully placed into the wall structures. They also display a high awareness of astronomy and are aligned to geographical points, solstices and equinoxes.

The discovery of the ancient stone calendar site by Johan Heine in among all these stone dwellings and temples, would suggest that some of the structures would date back to the same era as the calendar some 75,000 years ago. It shows us with a certain level of clarity that these lost civilisations have been around for much longer than anyone could ever have imagined. It would not be absurd to then suggest that we may be staring at the very first concentrated human settlements inhabited by the early Homo sapiens on planet Earth.

A great aerial view of the sprawling settlement with a road that connects the ruins. The road is on average 3-4 metres wide. This level of construction indicates a very large community with very specific needs for transporting something. What did this ancient civilisation need to transport all those years ago?

ANCIENT ROADS AND TERRACES

What is most puzzling is the construction of ancient roads that probably ran for hundreds of miles and still connect many of these ruins. Keep in mind that according to historians 'the wheel' only reached this part of Africa in the 15th century AD when the Portuguese and Dutch explorers began to show interest in this part of the world.

Elaborate terraces indicate a high agricultural activity, often resembling those of the Inca settlement at Machu Pichu in South America. Such terraces run for hundreds of kilometres along many of the stone structures in South Africa alone. It is imperative to excavate these terraces across a wide area to determine what kind of plants or produce these ancient people were cultivating. Dating of organic matter will be valuable in this regard. Is it possible that these were the earliest agricultural fields in human history?

If these dwellings were inhabited by ancient miners that date back thousands of years, maybe even 75,000 years ago like Adam's Calendar, why did they need roads? And what kind of transport did they use on these roads?

It is extremely difficult if not impossible to date rock from its natural erosion due to exposure to the elements of nature. Many of these ruins show no signs of human intervention since they were deserted. If the walls were originally 2,5 metres tall and one metre thick, how long would it take to erode down to 2 feet tall? Possibly hundreds of thousands of years.

Johan Heine firmly strapped into the seat of a helicopter, following his passion, exploring and documenting the countless ruins of southern Africa.

Stone dwellings and settlements interspersed with roads and terraces, boggle the minds of historians and archaeologists. Will we have to reconsider our understanding of human history and evolution in southern Africa?

Note that many of the internal circular structures either do not have entrances or have very small entrances.

Adam's Calendar | 27

A section of one of the many thousands of circular stone ruins in South Africa. This one displays a number of encoded symbolisms and must have played an important part in rituals and observations. There are a number of embedded rocks in the walls such as this circular shaped rock indicating east. The black reef shale rock is very hard and heavy. Most pieces are smooth around the edges indicating that they were obtained from an active river. The strange thing is, there is no such large river nearby.

VERY SPECIAL STONES

The flat smooth rock/slate used in the construction of the three ruins in this area is almost black, very hard and iron-like in its composition. Where did the builders get it from? Prof. Charlesworth from WITS University identified the rock as black reef shale that must have come from an active river because of its smooth edges. The closest river is small and weak and would not have been able to produce such an abundance of shale.

A small circular enclosure that makes up part of a larger ruin, puzzles historians and archaeologists. Possibly an observational chamber of some kind. Heavy black reef shale lie scattered around. What we do know is that these pieces are large and heavy. Some of the central rocks sticking out upright, are 1,4 metres tall. Where were they originally positioned and what role did they play? Was there an observational window looking east at the sunrise?

We need to perform a great deal of theoretical reconstruction to figure out these African mysteries. What we do need to avoid however, is the desecration of the sites through haphazard excavation, before the existing condition of the sites have been meticulously researched by open minded thinkers and not just a handful of conservative academics. The historical site at Mapungubwe in the Limpopo province of South Africa suffered a tragic blow when the original stone structures were demolished in the process of excavating the layers below. Thankfully there are a few old photographs and archaeological sketches showing that the surface rock formation was actually an observational calendar site. We could have learnt a great deal from first studying the rock placements of the site.

An example of the strange shapes of rocks scattered in the vicinity of the ruin.

Adam's Calendar | 29

Here we get an indication of the original height of the walls that still reach 2,5 metres in places. This section has an observational window that was strategically positioned to line up with other structures and marker stones inside the ruin. For what purpose? Most likely observing the sunrise and various aspects of it, as its general positioning is east.

Johan's presence indicates the sheer size if the walls that reach 1,5 metres in width in some places. It was no easy task building these walls. The specifically chosen black reef shale and the intricate construction with smaller rocks in the centre of the wall, once again show that this was a well planned operation. Where did they get the heavy, flattened rock from?

The narrow entrance to a famous ruin built in the shape of Hindu fertility symbol. Notice the width of the walls again. This is one of the ruins that brings to an end the notion that these were simply cattle kraal built by the Bantu people when they first settled here around 1300 AD.

Two more stone markers in the wall of this particular ruin indicate north.

A narrow entrance of less than 2 feet into the centre of the ruin indicates that this was no cattle kraal but an important venue for rituals and observations by its ancient architects.

An obviously placed marker stone sticks out of the ground hiding an ancient secret yet to be discovered. What is it telling us?

Adam's Calendar | 31

Many of the walls are not even in height, but rather show a purposeful wave shape along the top. We suspect that the position of the peaks and troughs in the walls could have observational relevance as well.

Dr. Cyril Hromnik from Cape Town has been studying these circular ruins for around 30 years. He was possibly the first historian researcher to find evidence of gold mining activity by Indian miners, as far back as 2000 years ago and possibly beyond. This is how he describes them:

"*MaKomati* - Until the 16th century the gold producing region of Mpumalanga was known as Komatiland. Early Portuguese sources describe it as **Terra dos Macomates**, the land of the Komati people. Komati was the professional name of a Dravidian merchant caste of South India. This name is still attached to the Komati River, Komatipoort, etc. During centuries of gold exploration they mixed with the indigenous Kung (Bushmen) creating the Quena (Otentottu), and with the Black people from the North West creating the aBantu people, and together they gave rise to the MaKomati. The pre-European form of the name was MaKomatidesa, Land of the MaKomati." (Hromnik, 1995)

This interesting feature could have two possible functions. Either as an observational seat looking over the ruins below; OR an altar for offerings.

THE BIGGEST SURPRISE

The flat smooth rock/slate used in the construction of the three ruins in this area is almost black, very hard and iron-like in its composition. Where did the builders get it from? Prof. Charlesworth from WITS University identified the rock as black reef shale that must have come from an active river because of its smooth edges. The closest river is small and weak and would not have been able to produce such an abundance of shale.

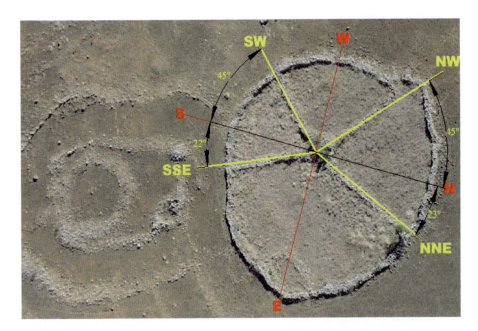

Most modern academics have been calling these circular stone structures cattle kraal, claiming that they were of no real historic importance. Hromnik and others had been insisting that they are much more than that. But to prove such crazy speculations they needed proof.

After measuring and analysing the ruins for years they finally found the proof to support such maverick views of the ruins. Using his professional architectural software and experimenting with the shapes and geometry of the ruins, Johan cracked the encoded alignments that have been meticulously worked into some of the structures.

The cattle kraal turned out to be very clever cattle kraal – obviously intended for very clever cattle.

Many of them show distinct geographic alignments with north, south, east and west; solstices and equinoxes. But only when Johan began to analyse the shapes, he discovered the incredible detail and depth of encoded geometry in their structure.

34 | Adam's Calendar

Adam's Calendar | 35

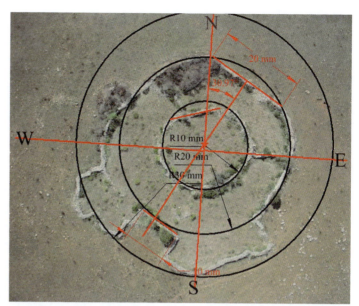

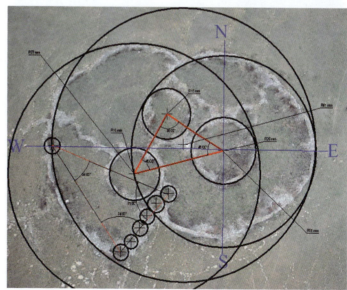

The Golden ration of Phi also known as the Fibonacci sequence of 1,618 is deeply encoded in the structures. This kind of mathematical consciousness has never been witnessed by any civilisation in southern Africa.

The entire cliff edge is filled with the carefully placed rocks as part of a giant observational arena. It is clear to see that they are not the same rock type as the bedrock, which was identified as black reef quartzite, which is rich in gold. The rocks on top are dolerite. An intrusive igneous rock from lava and volcanic activity.

THE KEY TO UNLOCKING THE ANCIENT PAST

But the key to all of these discoveries lies at the top of the mountain at the far end of this entire cliff edge. Adam's Calendar firmly places some of these ruins at a point in history that we modern humans have never faced before. Because if Adam's Calendar is 75,000 years old, some of these circular stone ruins must be the same age and even older. Because the people who lived here and toiled in the ancient gold mines, would have first built homes and temples before building an elaborate observational calendar site.

A closer look at an abandoned dolerite rock showing clear signs of possible carving. In the background we see the expanse of the cliff edge filled with scattered alignments of stone monoliths.

Adam's Calendar | 39

These rocks are not part of the bedrock and were brought here by someone at some point in history, and placed in their positions for a specific purpose.

Johan points out one of the many giant monoliths that show evidence of human carving and engraving. Many of the rocks along this ledge may have been placed in specific positions and are carefully grinded and sculptured into unique shapes. Some of these sculptured stones approximate human shapes.

Spectacular sunrise on a winter's morning over Adam's Calendar. This is how its builders would have seen it some 75,000 years ago.

THE CENTREPIECE

But the centrepiece of the mountain top is Adam's Calendar.

The carved edge can be clearly seen, resulting in a sharp edge to cast a clear shadow on the flat calendar rock. The wider monolith became the calendar on which days and weeks were marked as the movement of the sun stretched perfectly from one edge to the other, left to right, and then back again.

A wider view of the site showing some of the other rocks that make up numerous geographical alignments against a surreal blue sky.

Michael Tellinger uncovers another male shape monolith at the north site. It would stand about 2,5 metres tall.

46 | Adam's Calendar

THE SEARCH FOR ADAM

The so-called *'Cradle of Humankind'* at the Sterkfontein caves has been promoted aggressively but in truth it is really a misnomer. There are no human remains or ancestors at the Sterkfontein caves – but various hominid skeletons that date back over 3 million years. These creatures have absolutely nothing to do with humankind and only serve to confuse the masses by being called "Cradle of Humankind". Is the real cradle of humankind actually situated in Mpumalanga? Will the lost stone cities of southern Africa produce the human fossil evidence we have been searching for?

The oldest written records available to us today are the many thousands of Sumerian clay tablets that have been collected over several centuries from the middle East and Near East, otherwise known as the 'land between the rivers' or Mesopotamia. These tablets are written in a script called cuneiform that was first deciphered towards the end of the 1800s. They reveal to us many valuable clues about the first established civilisation in Sumer (Mesopotamia). Some of these tablets date back to over 3 000 years before the first books of the Bible were first written. In fact much of what has been written in the book of Genesis comes from its original form written on many of these clay tablets. Like; the story of creation; Adam and Eve; garden of Eden; Noah and the flood; tower of Babel; the story of Abraham; Sodom and Gomorrah, and more.

These tablets tell us that mankind was first created in what they call the Abzu, southern Africa. But it was not a tale of sunshine and happiness. As most historical scriptures seem to indicate, man's first love has always been gold.

A misty morning at Adam's Calendar.

HUMAN OBSESSION WITH GOLD

Human history cannot be separated from the quest for gold. Since the earliest of time man has been obsessed with gold and mined gold from the Earth in various ways. It is truly curious that Homo sapiens would be so concerned with this metal when they first walked the Earth, when their primary concerns should have been food, shelter and security. This does not however seem to be the case. As early as Genesis 2, even God displays his obsession for this shiny metal when he talks about the land of Eden, where there is gold. Soon after this God promises to take the people to the land of "milk & honey" where there was gold.

Entrance to an old gold mine lined with rocks that were obviously not of any interest to the miners.

Eroded soil and stone fills the bottom of the mine which is now about 20 metres deep. Trees and aloes have found the soft soil at the bottom a fertile place to grow.

The Sumerian tablets tell us that it was here in southern Africa that man's encounter with gold began when the early humans were forced to work as slaves in gold mines. Could this be linked to the huge complex of ancient stone settlements that stretch from Mpumalanga, South Africa, all the way to Kenya and possibly beyond?

These sprawling human settlements and stone structures in southern Africa may yet expose thousands of generations and many civilisations that were the first humans on Earth. This is the closest we have ever come to seeing the earliest human settlements in large communities with structures that point to a certain lifestyle and purpose – MINING GOLD.

Adam's Calendar becomes a crucial piece of what I call the 'Great Human Puzzle' as it brings us closer to the earliest humans on Earth and shows us how they lived and what they did, some 75,000 years ago and possibly even further back in time.

52 | Adam's Calendar

HOW THE CALENDAR WAS DISCOVERED

It was a late afternoon and all the spotter planes and other flying crew from the 'Working For Fire' team were coming in to land at the old Nelspruit airport. Lizette, the dispatcher on duty, noticed that one of the pilots was not accounted for.

After various attempts to track the missing pilot via radio communication failed, they realised that something was seriously wrong and dispatched a number of helicopters to follow his most likely fight path to find the pilot and his plane. Unfortunately the night was approaching rapidly and the frantic search effort during the last hour of daylight did not deliver any results.

The next morning began with a concerted effort to find pilot Bevan Harris who was still missing.

By midday the plane was spotted by hikers where it had gone down over the edge of a cliff and was caught by the thick vegetation. Pilot Bevan Harris managed to climb out along the branches and sat all night in the freezing cold on the open cliff face while nursing a broken hand.

On the way to the rescue site, Johan notices a strange collection of rocks at the edge of a cliff overlooking the crashed plane. Opposite: The Search and rescue team sprung into action and began to descend on the scene.

The search and rescue helicopter hovers above the crashed plane giving instructions to the stranded pilot on the cliff face.

If it was not for the thick vegetation on the side of the mountain the pilot would most certainly have fallen to his death.

The 2 large rocks are instantly visible, even from some distance. As you approach, they draw you in like a magnet, clearly announcing their significance.

After ensuring that all was under control with rescuing the pilot, Johan approached the strange looking rocks. This was the first photograph ever taken of the calendar site from the ground. Any observant visitor would see the many monoliths scattered around the site – some that have fallen over with time and others overgrown by vegetation or partially covered by soil. This was the point of no return and the beginning of a 4-year obsession to get the giant stones recognised for the role they played in ancient civilisations of southern Africa.

THE RESCUE MISSION BEGINS

While hauling the pilot to safety from about 20 metres down on the cliff face, the rescue team is oblivious of the ancient calendar site lurking in the background. The two giant rocks are clearly visible to those who have an eye for such things, and TV producer Mimi Brodie, who was photographing the rescue effort, has just such an eye. As soon as she could tear herself away from the rescue site she went over to photograph the unusual rocks close up.

Notice the 2 trees with 2 giant rocks sticking out of the ground between them. Other rocks all around the centrepiece are conspicuously placed in a predetermined order. This was clearly not a fluke of nature and Johan instinctively knew that they had found a very unique stone site. How unique… would only become clear some 4 years later after his continued persistence and determination, and enduring many rejections from historians and archaeologists.

Johan at the rescue site monitoring the team with video camera in hand. The stone calendar is just visible above the rescuers in the distance.

Adam's Calendar | 57

COMING BACK TO EXPLORE THE MONOLITHS

Mpumalanga is arguably the most scenic province of South Africa. With breathtaking mountains that seem to stretch forever, it is also the gateway to the Kruger Park and the warm Indian ocean of Mozambique. An undiscovered tropical paradise that many locals like to frequent.

The amazing thing is that the dense vegetation along the sides of mountains suddenly clears when you reach the tops, where it is generally replaced by fertile arable soil. The mountains are all linked together and you can virtually walk forever with very little vegetation getting in the way. It makes perfect sense why the early settlers in this part of the world would have set up their settlements along the mountain tops.

The rocky cliffs and densely overgrown vegetation of the mountainside is contrasted by the flat arable soil that covers the top of the mountain. But as you approach, it becomes evident that this is no ordinary mountain top. The entire edge of the mountain seems to be covered with rocks that have some kind of purpose in their layout, and different alignments become instantly evident.

It is important to note that all the rocks on top of the mountain seem to have been placed there. They do not appear to be part of any bedrock below and are simply embedded and carefully placed in the soft arable soil. Geologists confirm that the bedrock is black reef quartzite while the monoliths are dolerite.

At closer inspection it becomes evident that these rocks are not randomly scattered but rather form a conscious grouping of alignments. The wooden pole was placed there by Johan and its crucial significance will be revealed soon.

From a helicopter you notice Adam's Calendar instantly with its two signature monoliths sticking out of the ground at the far end of the mountain top. But equally important are the 3 large rocks at the edge of the cliff that had fallen over. Upon closer inspection it became evident that they once stood upright at the very edge pointing to some kind of stellar formation.

The positioning of the stones becomes very intriguing from the air, hinting at the distinct possibility that there may be some kind of astrological alignment hiding in its layout as well.

The large carved monolith becomes visible and beckons the question – who would have carved this stone and for what purpose?

Adam's Calendar | 65

Printed in Great Britain
by Amazon

Not Just Oxygen

© Calne Wordfest

All rights reserved

IBSN 9798325665370

Not Just Oxygen

An anthology celebrating the work of Joseph Priestley, natural philosopher

by Calne Wordfest Writers' Group and Friends

But it is only upon landing and closer inspection that you realise the effort which the builders of this site went to in carving out the monolith. It is extremely difficult to carve a large stone of this density with basic tools even today.

Below: The tree and the rock on the right, form the north marker.

Adam's Calendar | 67

And so began the clearing, measuring and calculating the various components of Johan's new obsession.

Right from the start Johan instinctively knew that he had discovered something special but he had no idea how special and significant his find really was. He began filming and calculating the various angles and alignments.

Even the clearing team stops to take in the view. It is truly spectacular and it makes absolute sense why the builders would have chosen this particular spot from all the surrounding mountain tops.

Adam's Calendar | 69

Once the site was cleared, Johan could come back on a regular basis and make a number of observations and measurements. Very soon he realised that this site was meticulously planned and much more complex that he had ever imagined. The task of observing the sunrise and sunset over a long period, began.

Adam's Calendar | 71

WAITING FOR THE SUNRISE!

Summer and winter, the sunrise had to be observed and recorded. In the photo on the left we also see a whole bunch of ORBS.

A spectacular winter sunrise over the monoliths. But the true angle of the rise of the sun had shifted. This would be a crucial bit of information when it came to dating the site.

What is interesting to note is how the top of the tall rock was flattened to match the contours of the horizon, allowing the sun to rise exactly in the middle. This angle was altered for dramatic effect because today the sun actually rises a few degrees away from the monolith.

Soon it became obvious that the large flat stone closer to the edge had a much more pivotal role to play in all this. It was not long before Johan realised that it was in fact the actual calendar surface on which the ancient people could mark the days and weeks of the year.

The setting afternoon sun casts a shadow on the calendar rock.

All the points of view at Adam's Calendar are dramatic. This winter sunset highlights two marker stones that cast a shadow on the flat monolith. The shadows can clearly be seen on the paper covering the monolith.

The flat rock was covered with paper so that Johan could trace the movement of the setting sun over an extended period. What he found was astounding.

The builders of the site had specifically carved the taller rock so that the sharp edge would cast a shadow on the flat rock. This shadow moves exactly from one edge of the flat rock across to the other side as the year goes by, allowing the people to create a calendar with markings on the surface.

Then, at the solstice, the shadow stops on the far edge of the rock and makes its way back to the other edge.

The amazing thing is the effort they made to carve and grind the one edge of the tall rock so that this measuring of the days could be accomplished accurately.

An angle from behind the flat monolith indicating the direction of the setting sun.

The alignments get more interesting. This is a view from the north marker towards the south marker as it dissects the monoliths exactly. The stone between the monoliths is another monolith that has fallen over. It seems to have been the central point between the north and south markers.

THE ALIGNMENTS BECOME QUITE OBVIOUS

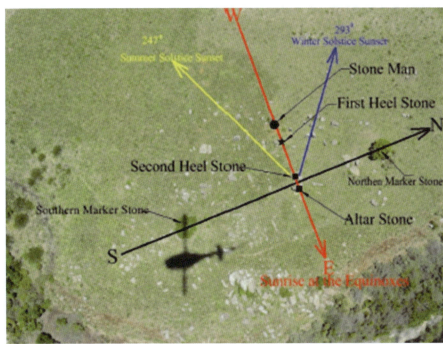

The tree on the right is the north marker. Tree on the left indicates south.

On the left: A close look at the North stone with the opportunistic growth of a tree next to it. Right: South marker stone that seems to have split in two and a tree grows out of the crack.

Adam's Calendar | 83

A moody misty view north east. Looking from the wooden pole across the monoliths, we face east.

Numerous wooden pegs are scattered throughout the entire site as testimony of Johan's ongoing measurements and observations.

Reverse-view confirming the perfect planning – the view from the south marker towards the north stone. The tree between the monoliths gives it away.

Adam's Calendar | 85

Johan explains how the shadow could also have been used to tell time from the descending shadow on the edge of the rocks. There seems to be a secondary purpose for the top edges of the flat rock.

Pointing out one of the many alignments as the shadow of the setting sun stretches over one of the rocks.

The shadow of a secondary marker stone falls on the main tall rock indicating the equinox.

Pondering the complexity of this ancient stone calendar. The fine edge of the shadow is clearly visible. The incredible thing about this kind of work is that every time you visit the rocks and spend time observing, you make a new discovery. And just when you think you are getting the hang of it… bad weather strikes, only to remind you how complex and time consuming the construction of a site like this truly is.

Adam's Calendar | 87

Located high on a mountain top the site is often covered by clouds and mist.

88 | Adam's Calendar

At least the mist provides a new atmosphere for dramatic photographs.

The only thing you can do is sit it out with a hot cup of coffee and wait for the cloud to clear. A luxury that the ancient builders probably did not have. Michael Tellinger and Johan Heine on one of the many exploratory visits to Adam's Calendar.

A TWIST IN THE TALE

When Johan was measuring and contemplating the various alignments he noticed a hole in a position directly aligned with the two main monoliths. Even more curious were the scrape marks on a rock adjacent to the hole. He wondered if there could have been a stone in that position at some point in time. This would have been a very important stone as its point of view was exactly east in line with the main monoliths. This stone would have marked the equinox sunrise.

Johan placed the wooden pole in the position where the 'stone man' was taken out. One can immediately see the alignment with the other monoliths facing due east at the sunrise during the equinox.

At that moment the local horse trail master, Christo Germishuys, came riding by and when Johan explained his puzzling dilemma to him about the missing stone, Christo's explanations resolved the mystery. Some 10 years before, in 1994, the amazing shape of the stone caught the attention of a group of bird enthusiasts. The large stone was roughly shaped in the form of a human being – anthropomorphic in its appearance. The large man-shaped stone was moved to a new place closer to the entrance of the reserve marking the official opening of the Blue Swallow Reserve. Little did they know that this was the oldest man-made statue on Earth and the centrepiece of the oldest man-made structure found to date.

Did this human shaped rock represent the first free human looking out at his first free sunrise some 75,000 years ago?

*Different views of what could possibly be the oldest and first man-made statue in human history. **'The Stone Man'**.*

Johan inspects the plaque on the stone man. This was the second plaque placed there. Notice the grinder marks above where the first plaque was forcibly removed by vandals because of its copper or bronze content.

Michael Tellinger hugging the oldest statue in the world. A truly spiritual experience.

Adam's Calendar | 93

The Stone Man looks east at the sunrise.

Adam's Calendar | 95

But Adam's Calendar keeps sprouting new surprises.

Looking between the branches of the trees that indicate north-south Johan noticed a tree in the distance about one kilometre away. Upon closer inspection we found that the tree was an opportunistic growing tree just like the other two that mark north and south.

The mysterious tree about 1 kilometre north of the main site is just visible. Could it hold some additional secrets linked to Adam's Calendar?

Inside many of the circular stone ruins of southern Africa there are smaller circular structures with a flat surface. They normally stand 2-3 feet high and a few feet in diameter, like the one inside the main court of Great Zimbabwe. Some historians believe that they could have been altars for offerings to the gods. Was this circular stone structure beneath the tree near Adam's Calendar the first altar for offerings to the ancient gods?

Whose seat was this? And what were they observing? Just one of the many breathtaking phenomena surrounding Adam's Calendar.

ONE GIANT ANCIENT OBSERVATORY

As we explored the rest of the mountain top we realised that this was not just an isolated site, but most likely a major ancient observatory with a number of sites serving a variety of observational needs. Everything and every rock seems to have a purpose and was placed in its spot by the ancient architects for very particular reasons. Unless of course they had so much time on their hands that they carried large rocks around the mountain top simply for fun?

It does not take a genius to realise that something strange has been going on, on this mountain ledge. Geologists confirm that many of these rocks have been manipulated and moved into place.

Many of the rocks and monoliths show distinct evidence of carving and an attempt to shape them into various forms.

This is probably not natural erosion but evidence of carving.

Johan inspects some of the many monoliths that have fallen over with time.

This particular one is a good example of carving and shaping into what seems to be another human shape.

Adam's Calendar | 105

Erosion has created some interesting shapes in several stones. This one caught our attention for its skull-like appearance. What is more important however is the indication of how long these rocks have been on the mountain top. For such hard rocks to erode to this level would take many thousands of years. Is this nature's work over 75,000 years?

This rock was carved and then split open.

Johan points out one of the many alignments. This one seems to be east.

Trees have caused much damage to the structure and layout of the ancient rocks. Here is one of the many examples of how the tree has caused one rock to split and the other to topple over from the root activity.

Adam's Calendar | 107

MALE AND FEMALE FORMS

When we first began to explore the main Adam's Calendar site, we were not too familiar with the shapes and meanings of the rocks. But with each visit we learn something new. Since discovering the other two sites, one to the south and the other to the north, we began recognising reoccurring shapes. Once we realised that the 'stone man' rock was removed from the main site, we began to notice other monoliths that also took on a human shape. Some resemble the 'stone man' which has a broad base, narrows down towards the neck and head and then has a round part which would symbolise the head – we call this the 'male' shape. The other shape has a big base section that narrows to a pointed section above it – 'female' shape.

A male shaped rock lies on its side. The rounded head or face part has broken off and is lying a few feet in front of it.

A male monolith found at the third site. About 2,5 m long but unfortunately it has also fallen over with time and probably the movement of the soil below.

The female rock which has also fallen over lies a few metres to the north of the male. This one carries signs of engraving just to add to the mystery.

A female shaped rock at the north site lies (some distance) to the north of the male. It has also begun to fall over but because of its wider base still remains partially upright.

Adam's Calendar | 109

Equinox sunrise 2007, showing the secondary marker stone (heel stone) closest to camera.

112 | Adam's Calendar

STRANGE MAGNETIC FIELDS

One of the fascinating things we noticed on one of our trips to Adam's Calendar was the strong magnetic field that surrounds the rocks. Different rocks show different amounts of magnetic activity when the compass is brought closer to its surface. The two big monoliths cause a 90 degree deviation on the compass when measured individually from the outer direction. But when we placed the compass in between them, it caused a full 180 degree swing. Did this magnetic property play a role in its original function? Why were such rocks with strong magnetic properties chosen?

When the compass is moved in between the two main rocks it swings a full 180 degrees.

Indivdual deviation is 90 degrees. The red hand of the compass should be facing north, towards the camera.

Adam's Calendar | 113

MORE TO EXPLORE

Once you start looking and your eyes are sensitised to these kinds of stone ruins, you begin to find all kinds of wonderful places. Fred took us to one such place in Mpumalanga. We call it the Stone Forest. Thousands of giant monoliths just standing upright as if they were receiving some kind of communication from space. It was truly a spiritual experience walking among them. There are amazing shapes of stone and many possible alignments with all kinds of geographic points, but it will require many hours and much exploration to begin understanding this site and its possible role in human history. Maybe, it is just a beautiful example of nature's many remarkable ways of showing itself – without any real significance.

Rocks do not erode into triangular shapes in nature, except a few rare "dreikanter" formations found in some deserts.

DATING THE STONES

One of the most difficult things to do when working with ancient stone ruins is to date them. Those that have studied the historic speculations around Stone Henge will be familiar with the many attempts and the various ways in which archaeologists and astronomers have gone about trying to pin an age to the megaliths at that site. The same can be said for all such structures found on Earth to this day. Even though there may have been some organic matter found at the site which is datable with various techniques, it cannot be assumed that such organic material was left there

The two trees are the focal points and allow us to measure the geographic deveation of north - south over time.

The slight deviation of the north - south markers to the left of twelve o'clock can even be seen in this satelite photo.

Adam's Calendar | 119

A number of large monoliths can be seen at the edge of the cliff where they fell over as the soil has moved towards the edge. Notice the pointed one on the right.

Johan inspects the fallen monoliths at the edge.

by the original builders. It may have been deposited thousands of years later by other users of the site.

Although there are various techniques that have been suggested, some of them being a form of magnetic resonance deviation dating, and analysing the rock content to work out when it may have been formed, these would simply not do the job. We had to turn to archaeoastronomy and astronomy itself for possible answers. And they certainly provided answers that surprised all of us. Archaeoastronomy can only be used if there was an originally intended alignment with sunrises, solstices and constellations. Because of the Earth's so-called wobble on its axis every 25,800 years, which is called precession, and the variation in axial tilt of Earth, which occurs in 41,000 - year cycles, astronomers can calculate the age of such a site from the deviation in the current alignment from the original alignment. So if the intended geographical point like north is not in line with the current north, it means that the site was built a long time ago. All we have to do is figure out how long ago.

Due to the ongoing exploration done by Johan Heine at the site, we could make such a comparison and we found that the intended original north, south, east, west markers were out of line by 3-5 degrees of arc counter clockwise.

The monolith facing the camera was clearly sculptured to a point.

This allowed astronomer Bill Hollenbach to determine that the site was built at least 25,000 years ago or multiples thereof.

We analysed human activity in ancient times to try and make some sense of it all. Could this site be older than 25,000 years?

After Anthony Stevens measured and surveyed the site he found the deviation in alignments to be 3 degrees 17 minutes 42 seconds, from the originally intended alignments by the ancient builders. This allowed us to get a second opinion from an astronomer who concluded that the site is probably much closer to 75,000 years old.

But we wanted to corroborate our dating techniques so we asked another astronomer to analyse the curious positioning of the three giant rocks at the edge of the cliff. It seems that these rocks were once upright, pointing to a stellar alignment in antiquity. Our question was simple. Which group of 3 stars would have been visible just before the sunrise at the equinox some 75,000 years ago?

The answer came back swiftly and resolute. Orion's Belt would have been lying perfectly flat on the horizon at that time in history. It would have been a spectacular site to behold just before the sunrise. The surveyor's illustration also revealed some new information not visible even from the helicopter shots. The entire site was once a large circle of monoliths, similar in a way to Stone Henge, with the 2 large calendar monoliths forming the central focal point.

Adam's Calendar | 121

The extension of the northern alignment runs directly into the lone tree and stone altar about a kilometre north of the site.

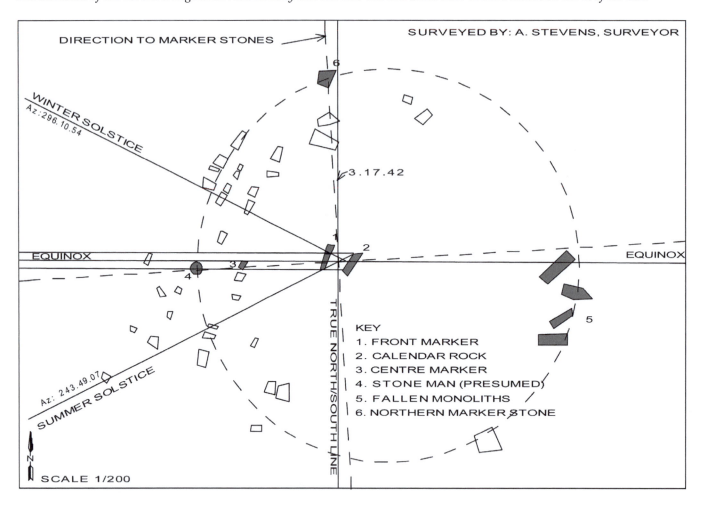

Equinox view.

Summer solstice view.

Winter solstice view.

The strange thing is that the earliest signs of human consciousness is set at about 80,000 years ago. This is when the Khoisan people of southern Africa began to paint a variety of images on the walls of caves in huge numbers. For explorers like myself it is overwhelming to find new previously unexplored caves and other ruin sites almost on a weekly basis. It is astonishing to see the emergence of these caves and the cave paintings in such large numbers at this time in our history. But the most mystifying thing is that prior to this we can find very little evidence of human activity on this planet. What the evidence points to however, is that mankind has been involved in mining activity from his earliest appearance on this planet. We will deal with the multitude of ancient goldmines in our next book.

Our assertion is that whatever the circumstances were for the earliest Homo sapiens on Earth, they were most certainly mining gold. But, it was not just any kind of mining, it seems that it was highly controlled, and the humans were somehow enslaved to do this mining for the first 200,000 years of their existence on this planet. There is simply no historic or scientific evidence found that contradicts this theory.

From the aerial shots that we present in this book, and that we will expand upon in a separate book, it is evident that these humans lived in concentrated communities here in southern Africa, mining for gold. But gold only became a valuable sought-after commodity many thousands of years later. It is difficult to imagine that the early humans would have done this unless they were forced to do so.

It is for these reasons that there is very little evidence of human activity prior to the 80,000-year mark. Then suddenly the evidence of humans is everywhere and within a short space of a few thousand years we find humans scattered all over the planet. Is it possible that this was the moment in our history that the gold-mining humans of southern Africa were somehow released or liberated and allowed to roam the world?

This would also correspond with the other common denominator that humans have shared since the earliest of time – slavery. As far back as we can trace humankind, we have been mining gold and practicing slavery.

So, what does this all mean? It means that this Adam's Calendar was most likely built by this same group of early humans when humankind was first liberated from the gold mines some 75,000 years ago.

It therefore symbolises the FIRST FREE HUMAN looking at his FIRST SUNRISE as a free species on planet Earth.

FOR THE MYSTICS

The past decade has seen a rapid increase in the use of mystics to solve crimes and profile criminals. Police investigative teams have had great success with this unconventional methodology and inadvertently have given psychics a new level of credibility. Micki Pistorius is South Africa's most famous criminal profiler with an unquestionable history of success. With her psychic abilities she has helped the SA police solve many complex crimes. Should we continue to be sceptical and cynical towards people with such abilities? We asked three individual psychics about the age of Adam's Calendar and they all replied that it was between 75,000 and 80,000 years old.

Nicola Wilson is a local resident who has been visiting the site for decades. As a school girl she and a group of friends would go sit at the site while bunking school and she has many fascinating stories to tell about the site.

Horses would never want to go near the centre. In the morning the grass in the centre would often be flattened while the grass on the outside of the central stone collection would stand perfectly upright.

On many occasions, they witnessed strange lights hovering above the site or moving around in the vicinity.

Several years ago Nicola found an old pot in a cave nearby which was dated by the Barberton museum to about 1500 BC. When she came to claim the pot back, so that it could be returned to where it came from, she was refused and has not been able to retrieve it since. This only goes to indicate that this site has probably been used by many civilisations over thousands of years for various reasons.

To push the realm of possibility even further, some of Nicola's 'weird' acquaintances have suggested that the site is actually an active portal for off-world beings to come and go. The strange thing is, that all three individual psychics we approached with the images of the site said exactly the same thing. Should we believe them? In 1982 Bradley Lee took a photo at the site and when the negatives were developed, they saw a "smoke figure" in the shot between the rocks.

Bradley examined the negative but it showed no signs of any such smoky figure. Every time they printed the picture however, the same smoke figure would appear. It is not very visible on the old faded picture now, but those readers with special intuitive and psychic powers will certainly see it and feel it. Enjoy it and please email us with your interpretation of the smoky figure so that we can get to understand it better.

Picture by Bradley Lee

128 | Adam's Calendar

Printed in Great Britain
by Amazon